P9-BJW-725

TOUCH, TASTE AND SMELL

The Human Body

TOUCH, TASTE AND SMELL

Brian R. Ward

Series consultant:
Dr A. R. Maryon-Davis
MB, BChir, MSc, MRCS, MRCP

The Human Body

Franklin Watts
London New York Sydney Toronto

Reprinted 1983

First published in Great Britain 1982
Franklin Watts Limited
12a Golden Square
London W1

First published in the United States of America by
Franklin Watts Inc.
387 Park Avenue South
New York, N.Y. 10016

UK edition: ISBN 0 85166 947 6
US edition: ISBN 0-531-04460-2
Library of Congress Catalog Card No: 82-50058

Designed by Howard Dyke

Phototypeset by Computape (Pickering) Ltd, North Yorkshire
Printed in Great Britain by Springbourne Press, Essex

Acknowledgments

The illustrations were prepared by: Andrew Aloof, Marion
Appleton, The Diagram Group, Howard Dyke, Hayward Art
Group, David Holmes, David Mallott.

Contents

Introduction 6

Senses and the brain 8

The sensitive skin 10

The sense of touch 12

Depending on touch 14

Heat and cold 16

Feeling pain 18

Preventing pain 20

Monitoring the muscles 22

Taste and smell 24

The organs of smell 26

How we detect smells 28

The sensitive nose 30

The organs of taste 32

How taste works 34

Fooling the senses 36

Glossary 38

Index 40

Introduction

Touch, taste and smell are important senses in our everyday life. Touch is a protective sense. It tells us when we are close to danger, or in contact with something which could cause injury.

In primitive times smell and taste were also protective. They told us which foods were good or safe to eat, backing up information passed to the brain from the eyes. Now we need not rely so much on smell and taste to tell us if something is edible.

Instead, taste and smell, together with touch, are responsible for our enjoyment of the food we eat. The characteristic taste, smell and texture of food allow us to identify each part of a meal. We usually group all these three senses together and call them "taste," but in reality each is quite distinct. The "taste" we experience is the result of the brain putting together information received from several different types of sense organs.

Our appreciation of "taste" changes throughout life. Young children prefer bland foods, while adults usually learn to enjoy strong-tasting and smelly foods such as mature cheese, garlic, onions and pepper. In the elderly the senses are less effective, so even stronger "tastes" may be needed to provide the same enjoyment of food.

We have a well-developed sense of temperature, which helps us to keep the body at an even temperature. It lets us know when to put on more clothes, if we are cold, and when to take them off, if we are overheated.

6

When we eat, we make use of many senses simultaneously. Taste and smell combine to give food its characteristic flavor. Temperature and touch are also important, and affect our enjoyment of food. The ability to enjoy strong-tasting or pungent-smelling foods is learned. Most children prefer mild tastes.

Senses and the brain

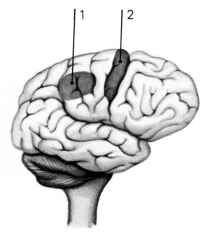

Different types of sensation are handled by particular areas on the surface of the brain.

1 shapes and textures are recognized at the sides of the brain

2 sensations of touch received on the surface of the body are recognized in a band across the top of the brain

The sensory cortex
The relative importance of different senses can be seen by measuring the area they take up on the surface of the cortex. The large area taken up by hands, face and eyes can be clearly seen.

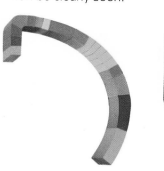

All information from the body's sense organs is passed directly to the brain along nerves. This information is carried in the form of tiny bursts of electrical energy, jumping from one cell to the next. It reaches the brain as a coded message, which has to be sorted out and understood.

Information from all the senses, including the eyes and ears, passes straight into a small area of the brain called the **thalamus**. The only exception is information from the organs of smell, which enters the front of the brain.

The thalamus, roughly in the middle of the brain, sorts out the incoming information and sends it to the **cortex**, or surface of the brain.

organs
tongue
mouth area

face
nose
eyes
fingers

hands
arms

trunk

legs
toes
genitals

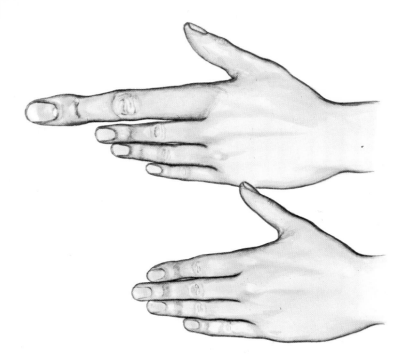

The cortex is deeply folded, giving it a very large area, so that it can cope with all the information it receives. Different parts of the cortex receive information from each set of sense organs. These regions are ranged across the brain's surface like the segments of an orange. The size of the area of cortex that is used for this is in proportion to the importance of the sense. Smell is restricted to a small area of the side of the brain, and taste also takes up a small area. But touch covers a wide band across the brain, and sensitive areas of the body such as the hands and lips take up a very large part of the cortex.

All these parts of the cortex are linked together by **nerve fibers**, allowing the senses to be "mixed" to give an overall impression of the world we live in.

This picture is distorted to show how the brain "sees" the sensitive fingers. The sense of touch in the fingers is so important that a large part of the brain is used to monitor the sense of touch in this region.

The sensitive skin

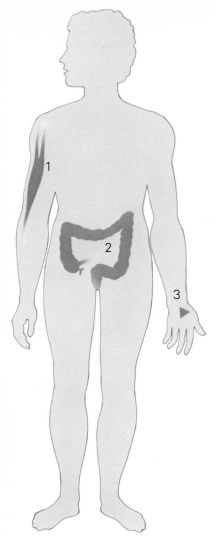

1 Stretch receptors in muscles monitor the position of the limbs.
2 Receptors in the digestive system monitor the passage of food.
3 Touch receptors, dotted over most of the surface of the skin.

The sense of touch is based on special receptors in the skin. There are other touch receptors inside the body, which act to help the automatic functions of our organs.

Our skin continuously passes huge amounts of information to the brain. The skin measures touch, pressure, pain, and temperature and gives the brain a constant picture of how each **stimulus** is affecting the body.

We react quickly to touch and pain, but the sensations of pressure and temperature are handled differently by the brain. Unless there is something special to report, information on pressure and temperature is simply recorded and "filed away," without our even becoming aware of the sensations.

Sensations are measured in the skin and other parts of the body by special organs called **receptors**. These are tiny structures at the end of hair-like nerve fibers. Many are rounded or button-shaped, and there are at least six different types, which are specialized according to the sensation they record.

When stimulated, a receptor can only produce a simple response. It is either "off" or "on," and each time it is switched "on," the receptor generates a pulse of electricity. The brain measures sensation according to the number of separate pulses generated by each receptor.

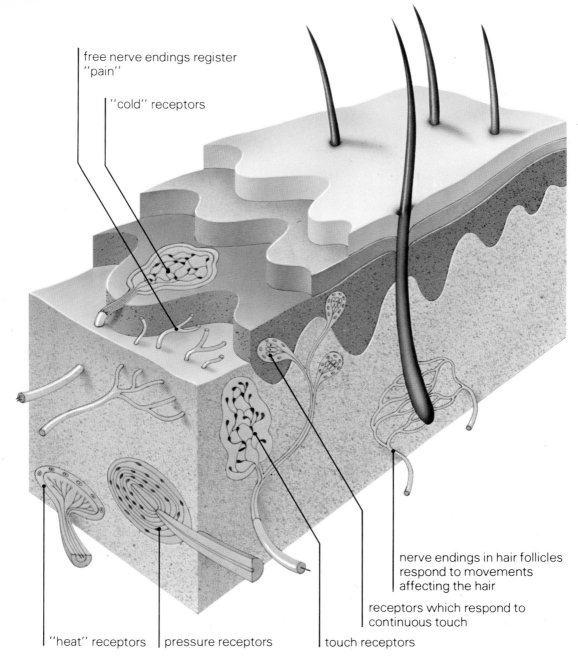

free nerve endings register "pain"

"cold" receptors

nerve endings in hair follicles respond to movements affecting the hair

receptors which respond to continuous touch

"heat" receptors | pressure receptors | touch receptors

Receptors are grouped together according to the importance of their function. The skin of the hands and face contains very large numbers of receptors and is particularly sensitive to touch.

A wide range of sensations are recorded in the skin. There are several different types of receptor, each with a specialized job, and these are positioned at different levels within the skin.

11

The sense of touch

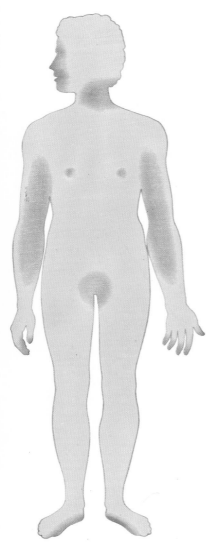

Touch and pressure are similar sensations, but there are different skin receptors for each. These receptors contain several layers of jelly-like material. When the receptors are squeezed, the layers inside them slide across each other to generate the nerve impulse.

Touch receptors are grouped very closely together on the tip of the tongue and the fingertips, which are extremely sensitive. On the back of the hand, however, the receptors are widely separated. You can prove this for yourself by using a pair of dividers. Touch one point gently on your skin. Then see how close you can get the other point before they both feel like a single point. On the fingertip, this is usually about $1/12$ in (2 mm); on the back of the hand it is about $2^1/_2$ in (60 mm).

This is because we rely very strongly on our fingertips to make us aware of the shape and texture of objects we touch. A blind person can even learn to read using the fingertips to decipher the 63 **Braille** characters, which consist of patterns of raised dots on the paper.

The fine hairs covering our body aid our sense of touch. They have receptors in their roots. When the hairs are stirred by even a slight breeze, they act as amplifiers to stimulate the receptors.

Touch receptors are grouped about the skin, depending on how sensitive the area needs to be. The areas shaded in green are the most sensitive places, where the receptors are clustered very closely together.

12

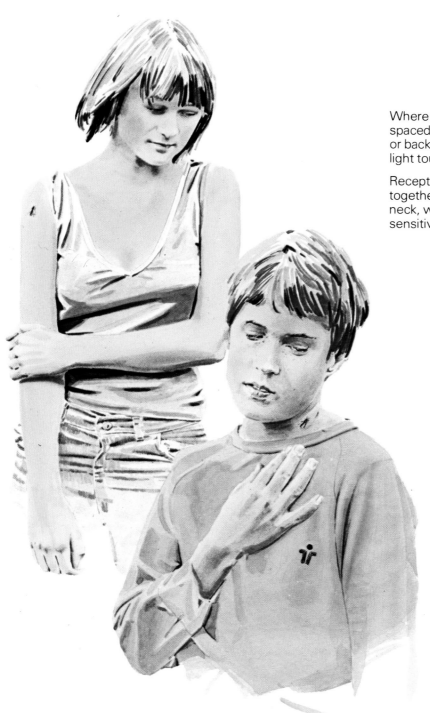

Where receptors are widely spaced, as on the upper arm or back, we may not notice a light touch.

Receptors are grouped close together on the face and neck, which are especially sensitive to touch.

Depending on touch

The senses of touch and pressure are important in protecting the body from injury, as are the related senses of temperature and pain.

When we exert ourselves to grip something tightly, we possess sufficient muscle power to damage the skin, or even to tear the **tendons** that attach our muscles to bones. Pressure receptors monitor the amount of force we use, and prevent such self-inflicted injury.

Without a sense of touch, we would soon damage ourselves severely. In the disease **leprosy**, nerves are damaged and sensation is lost in the affected parts. People suffering from the disease sometimes injure themselves because they cannot feel the warning sensations of touch and pressure.

We produce a mental "map" of our bodies, which means that the brain is aware of where each part of the body is positioned at any time.

It is so accurate that when a person has had a limb amputated, they can often "feel" it as though it were still there. These "phantom" limbs may itch, feel hot or cold, or be painful. All these sensations are probably due to scar tissue forming, stimulating the severed ends of the nerves which send false information to the brain.

This simple experiment shows how the "mental map" we have of our body can be tricked by an unusual situation. If the fingers are crossed, and a pea or other small object gripped between them, it feels as if we are holding *two* separate objects. The brain cannot envisage that a single object can touch the opposite sides of two fingers.

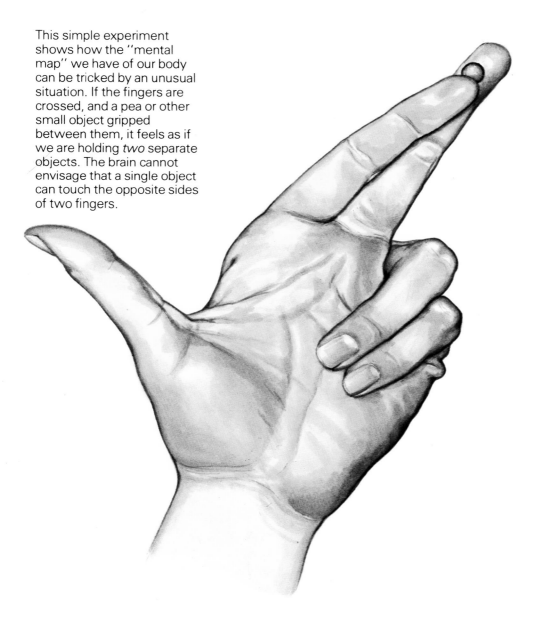

Heat and cold

For any warm-blooded creatures such as human beings, it is essential that the body is maintained at the proper temperature. We need to know the temperature outside our bodies so that we can keep our internal temperature constant by generating heat or getting rid of excess heat. The senses dealing with temperature alert the brain so that it can divert blood away from the skin to prevent heat loss, or increase blood flow to the skin to increase heat loss.

Temperature receptors seem to respond to *changes* in temperature, rather than to the temperature itself. This is why we are so sensitive to a cool draft in a warm room. We are conscious of a temperature drop of only one or two degrees, but less sensitive to a slight increase in temperature.

This can be demonstrated by a simple experiment, illustrated opposite, in which two fingers are dipped into the same glass of water. One will feel hot, the other cold. This is one of the many ways in which the senses can be tricked by situations which we do not normally encounter.

A simpler example results from the different spread of temperature receptors in the mouth and on the fingertips. The mouth contains very few temperature receptors, so we are able to drink coffee or tea at a temperature which would be extremely painful to the finger. Dip a finger into a cup of coffee to prove the point!

We become used to a temperature after a few minutes, and it may take a while to adjust to a different temperature.

Cold water

Dip a finger into icy water. At first it feels very cold, but after a few minutes it seems less cold.

Water at room temperature

Now dip the same finger into ordinary tapwater. It feels much warmer.

Water at room temperature

Dip another finger into the same water. The first finger still feels warm, but the second finger feels cold.

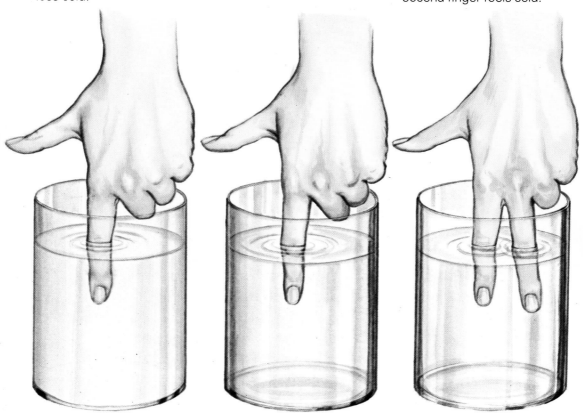

Feeling pain

The experience of pain is the most valuable of the protective senses. The sensation of pain can be caused by over-stimulation of ordinary pressure and temperature receptors, but there are also special pain receptors in the skin, in many internal organs and elsewhere throughout the body.

There are various types of pain, usually described as pricking, burning, itching and aching. Which one of these is felt seems to depend on how strongly the nerve endings are stimulated.

Sensitivity to pain varies throughout the body, depending on how many receptors are present. They are positioned quite differently to those for touch and temperature. Pain receptors are clustered thickly on the surface of the eye, which is why dirt in the eye is so painful. This causes us to blink rapidly to clear dirt from the eye's surface. On the fingertips, however, where we need large numbers of touch receptors, there are only a few pain receptors, which might otherwise interfere with our sense of touch. This means that the amount of pressure needed to cause pain in the fingertip is 1,500 times as great as that causing pain to the eye, and three times as great as that causing pain on the back of the hand.

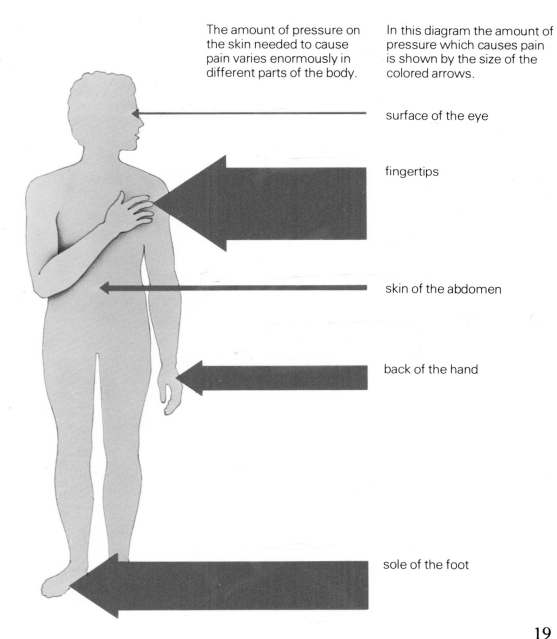

The amount of pressure on the skin needed to cause pain varies enormously in different parts of the body.

In this diagram the amount of pressure which causes pain is shown by the size of the colored arrows.

surface of the eye

fingertips

skin of the abdomen

back of the hand

sole of the foot

Preventing pain

Pain is a useful warning of possible damage to the body, but is often a nuisance when a false signal is produced, as sometimes happens with a headache.

Pain receptors send messages along nerves into the **spinal cord** and then up to the brain. Under some circumstances the brain has more important things on which to concentrate, so a special mechanism works to prevent the pain being experienced immediately. This may happen in sports, when athletes need to exert themselves so violently that it becomes painful. They must push on through the "pain barrier."

The mechanism which controls the experience of pain takes place alongside the spinal cord. Signals are sent down the spinal cord and into small groups of nerve cells called **ganglia**, where they intercept the incoming pain signals. They may shut off the signals completely, or let only some through to reach the brain.

We can feel how this works when we anticipate pain – for example when we go to see the dentist – and the mechanism is "switched off." When we are distracted by some other activity, the mechanism is switched on, and we may not even notice the pain until we relax later on.

A boxer must train himself to overcome pain which we would normally find distressing.

Monitoring the muscles

Another important group of sensory organs are called **proprioceptors**. These are receptors which monitor the condition and position of our body.

All muscles, tendons and joints are penetrated by nerves carrying proprioceptors, which respond mainly to the amount of stretch. As a muscle stretches or relaxes, it conveys an exact picture of its movement and position to the brain, helping us construct the "mental map" which is so important in everyday life.

A joint contains special receptors which give information about the position of the limb.

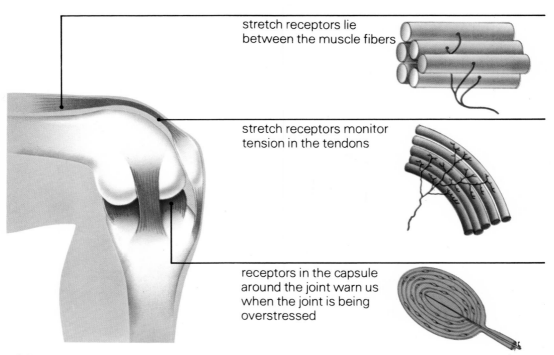

stretch receptors lie between the muscle fibers

stretch receptors monitor tension in the tendons

receptors in the capsule around the joint warn us when the joint is being overstressed

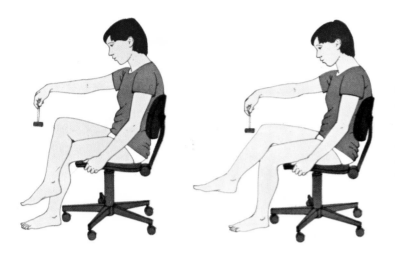

When the tendon just below the knee is tapped sharply, it is stretched slightly. This causes the receptors to send false information to the brain, which attempts to "correct" the position of the leg by causing it to kick.

Proprioceptors in the muscles also have an automatic function in helping us maintain our position effortlessly. A simple mechanism called a **reflex** helps control the position of fingers, arms, legs and most of the rest of the body. If part of the body shifts, its muscles are stretched, and this movement is noted by the proprioceptors. In the reflex this signal passes into the spinal cord, then back to the muscles, telling them to contract or relax to adjust the position of the body.

In the knee-jerk illustrated opposite, the blow to the knee stretches the proprioceptors in a tendon, so the body "believes" that the leg has been shifted. A reflex action makes a "correcting" movement, causing the leg to kick.

This reflex mechanism also works when we are moving about, smoothing muscular action and preventing jerky movements.

Taste and smell

Taste and smell are closely related sensations. Almost everything we taste, we also smell. This is due to the structure of the mouth and **nasal cavity** behind the nose. "Taste" takes place in the mouth, while organs of smell are situated in the nasal cavity.

We detect smells in the air breathed in or sniffed by the nose. When we are eating, however, microscopic particles of food, or food substances that have been dissolved in the droplets of water vapor from the moist saliva, float in the air within the mouth and throat.

Some of this air, together with the flavor-producing particles it contains, rises from the mouth through the gap behind the **soft palate** and into the nasal cavity. There it stimulates the organs of smell.

So the senses of taste and smell work together as we eat or drink, and the brain registers a single sensation.

Taste and smell are said to be primitive senses, which act on parts of the brain responsible for our most basic instincts, such as hunger, thirst and fear. Taste and smell can also have powerful emotional effects, awakening long-forgotten memories or causing changes in mood.

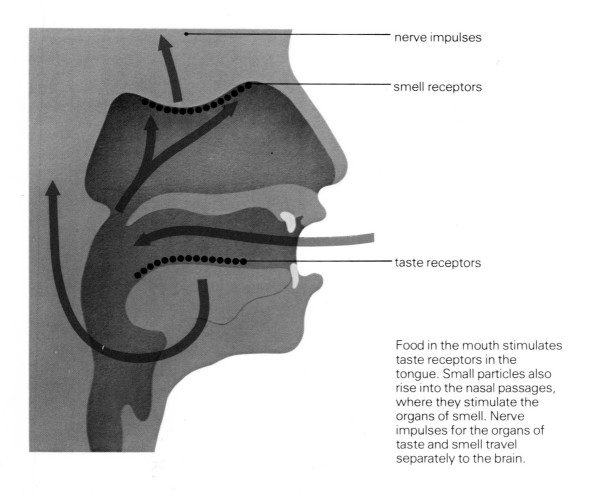

nerve impulses

smell receptors

taste receptors

Food in the mouth stimulates taste receptors in the tongue. Small particles also rise into the nasal passages, where they stimulate the organs of smell. Nerve impulses for the organs of taste and smell travel separately to the brain.

The organs of smell

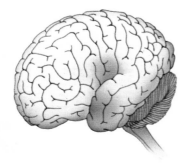

The sense of smell is recorded in a small area on the surface of the brain.

1 In normal breathing air passes directly into the back of the throat.

2 When we sniff, air eddies upwards and flows over receptors in the top of the nasal passages.

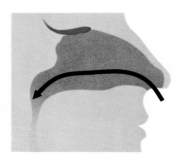

1

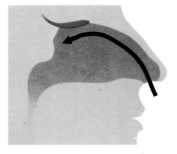

2

In the front of the skull, just behind the nose, is a large space called the nasal cavity. Air is drawn into and through the nasal cavity as we breathe.

Normally, this air passes straight across the floor of the cavity, down into the throat past the soft palate and is taken into the lungs.

Along the sides of the cavity are ledges of bone called **turbinates**. These channel the air in a direct flow, but they also allow some air to eddy, or circulate, to the top of the chamber. This small amount of circulated air comes into contact with the **olfactory organs**, the organs of smell.

The olfactory organs consist of patches of special receptor cells, connected to nerve fibers running directly into the brain. The receptors have sensory hairs which are embedded in a layer of sticky **mucus**. The sensory hairs can detect odors.

In order for us to notice a smell, the substance must be able to pass through the mucus to trigger off a response in the receptor cells.

Most of the nasal cavity is lined with mucus-secreting cells. There are also cells that have hairs called **cilia**, which beat continuously back and forth, producing a current in the mucus layer which covers

26

them. This helps to trap inhaled dust, and disposes of it in the mucus. This is then passed back into the throat and is swallowed.

The sense of smell is based on the function of the respiratory system. It is working continuously while we are breathing.

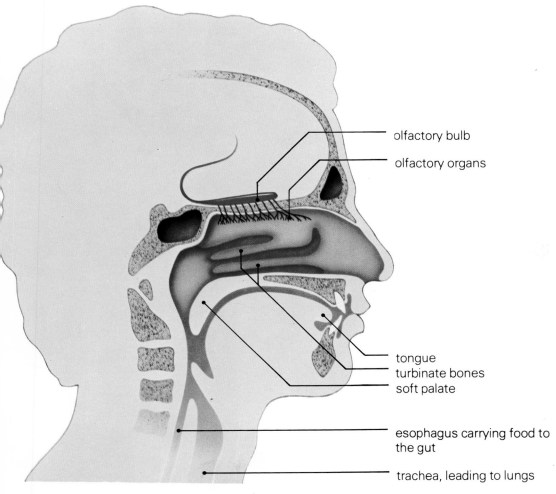

olfactory bulb

olfactory organs

tongue
turbinate bones
soft palate

esophagus carrying food to the gut

trachea, leading to lungs

How we detect smells

Normal breathing through the nose allows us to detect most smells, but when we really need to use our sense of smell, we sniff sharply. This causes the inhaled air to rush up into the upper part of the nasal cavity and stimulate the 50 million or more receptor cells.

No one is quite sure how smell is detected by the receptors. It is thought that receptors can only be triggered by substances with molecules of the right shape and size. These would fit into the receptor like a key in a lock.

This could explain why some quite different chemicals smell similar – their molecules happen to be of similar shapes.

Each receptor can respond to only one type of smell, yet we can distinguish thousands of different smells. It has been suggested that most smells are simply mixtures of about fourteen basic odors, each of which has a special receptor. So any particular smell would consist of a simple coded message from a combination of receptors, with some switched off and others stimulated to produce a signal.

It is thought that ''smelly''
substances are made up of
molecules which have a
characteristic shape. These
latch on to a particular type of
receptor, causing it to
produce a nerve impulse.

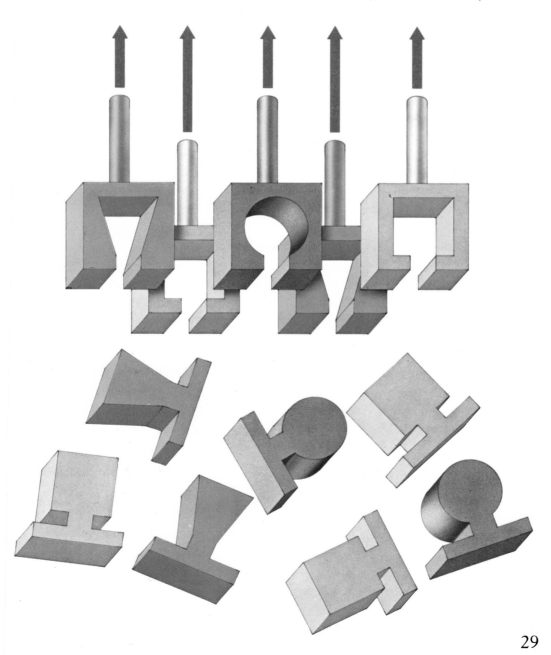

29

The sensitive nose

The human sense of smell is particularly sensitive to small numbers of molecules of "smelly" substances. It takes about eight molecules to trigger off a nerve impulse, but forty or more nerve impulses are needed before a "smell" signal is registered by the brain. Even then, we might not notice the signal consciously.

However, it takes only one molecule in every 50,000 molecules of inhaled air for us to detect a substance called **mercaptan**, which smells like rotten eggs. One intake of breath would leave a layer of mercaptan 1 molecule thick over the receptor cells.

Our sense of smell is very poorly developed compared to that of a dog, which is one million times more sensitive to certain smells. A dog's ability to detect its owner's smell is well known. A dog can follow a scent trail several days old, when only a few molecules of its owner's perspiration can be present.

Humans, like most animals, produce chemicals called **pheromones** in perspiration, which can act as scent messengers. Pheromones may play a part in sexual attraction, as well as in the recognition of a familiar person by their smell, although we are never consciously aware of their presence.

The dog's sense of smell is incredibly sensitive. Trained dogs can track a pérson's scent trail even after several days, and can detect a person buried under snow. Dogs are regularly used to find skiers buried under avalanches.

The organs of taste

Like smell, taste is a chemical sense, in which receptors are stimulated by substances in contact with them.

The organs of taste are called **taste buds**, and they are grouped on the upper surface of the tongue, on the soft palate, and in the back of the mouth.

An adult has nearly 10,000 taste buds, and an infant has many more, even covering the inside of the cheeks. In an adult most are grouped around the edges of the tongue and on the soft palate.

Taste buds are egg-shaped, and consist of a group of slim receptor cells arranged like orange segments. They open on to the

Taste receptors are called taste buds. They are grouped together on structures called papillae, which can be seen on the surface of the tongue as small bumps or specks.

 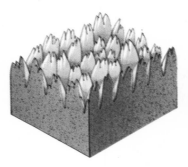 

tongue's surface through a small pore. Taste buds are grouped together in structures called **papillae**. The largest are shaped like little towers, each surrounded by a groove. Others are of various shapes, depending where they are situated, and they give the tongue its characteristic rough texture.

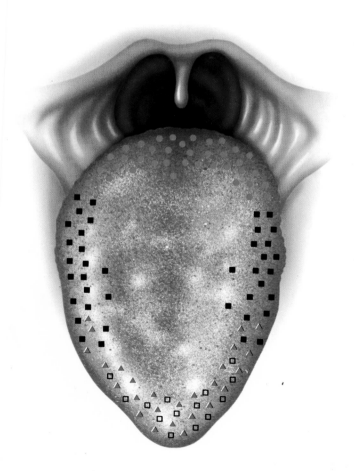

The organs of taste are located mostly on the surface of the tongue. They are grouped according to the tastes they perceive. Sweet and salt are registered at the front of the tongue, sour at the sides, and bitter at the back.

How taste works

The sense of taste is better understood than the sense of smell. It is known that we can identify four basic tastes – sweet, sour, salt and bitter. All flavors are made up of a combination of these four.

Different tastes are measured in separate areas of the mouth. The taste buds on the tip of the tongue register sweet and salt. Sourness is measured at the sides of the tongue, and bitterness is measured at the back of the tongue. This is why we quickly taste sugar or salt when we put food into our mouths, but get a bitter "aftertaste" only as we swallow.

Dissolved chemicals in food and drink probably fit on to the receptors in a similar way to those in the organs of smell. Saliva helps these substances to dissolve. But unlike all the other senses, taste is slow to register on the brain, and it may be several seconds before we identify a flavor.

Taste can be affected by other sensory properties of food or drink. The temperature of food or drink has a drastic effect on taste. Warm drinks taste sweeter than cool drinks, and bitterness is increased by coldness.

Similarly, the physical consistency of food affects our perception of a meal. Sometimes pain plays a part in taste, as in curries,

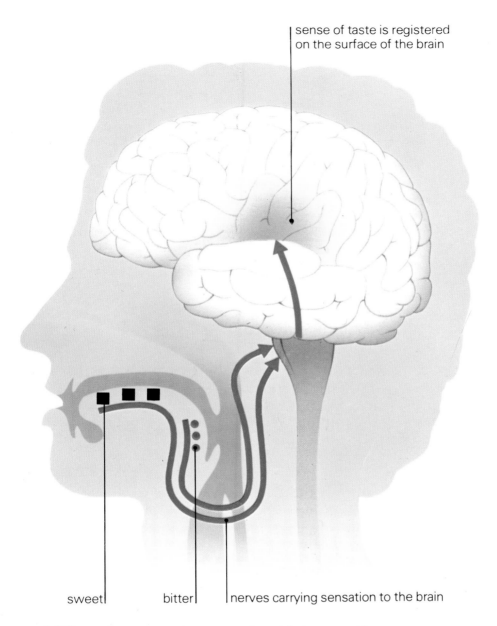

sense of taste is registered on the surface of the brain

sweet

bitter

nerves carrying sensation to the brain

chillies, pepper and mustard, which actually stimulate pain receptors in the mouth.

Salt is important in many foods. It seems to enhance unrelated tastes, as do several other substances commonly added to convenience foods.

Sweet and bitter can be experienced when drinking coffee with sugar. Each sensation travels to the brain along different nerves, and they are combined to form the single flavor that we experience.

35

Fooling the senses

All information picked up by our sense organs is sorted out and interpreted in the brain before we become consciously aware of its presence. The brain interprets the information in the light of previous experience. When a taste, smell, or combination of the two does not match up with its expectations, an incorrect interpretation may be made.

A yellow drink that tastes of strawberries will not be identified correctly, because we expect something yellow to taste of lemon. In this particular drink we will be able to tell that it is made of some kind of fruit but will not be able to identify the exact taste.

We also rely heavily on the sense of smell in identifying food. This is made obvious when we have colds, and inflammation and a heavy layer of mucus in our noses interfere with the sense of smell. All tastes then become deadened or distorted.

You can demonstrate this easily by putting on a blindfold, holding your nose, and getting someone to feed you a slice of apple, followed by a slice of potato. It is not usually possible to distinguish the two. Both apple and potato will taste sweet, but neither has a distinctive taste without the help of smell to complete the identification.

The sense of smell is essential in identifying most flavors. If you hold your nose while blindfolded, it is impossible to distinguish between apple and potato. Breathe in through your nose, and the proper flavor becomes immediately apparent.

Another experiment to demonstrate the importance of smell is to put a tiny drop of vegetable oil on the surface of a cup of coffee or tea. This will form a skin which prevents the escape of the vapor giving the drink its special flavor.

Glossary

Braille: special form of printed "writing" developed to allow the blind to read. Consists of patterns of raised dots making up letters and words.

Cilia: tiny hairs which beat back and forth, creating a current in the fluid covering them. Cilia help to keep the air passages clean.

Cortex: the pale gray surface layer of the brain, in which information is processed. Much of the brain's activity takes place in the cortex.

Ganglia: small groups of nerve cells, in which some information can be processed and acted upon, without involving the brain. Some reflexes are controlled in ganglia near the spine.

Leprosy: disease usually occurring in the tropics, in which bacteria damage the nervous system. Can result in serious damage to the hands and legs, due to its effect on the senses of touch, pain and temperature.

Mercaptan: one of the "smelliest" substances known. Just a few molecules of mercaptan can be detected by our sense of smell. Its smell resembles bad eggs.

Mucus: sticky, watery material secreted from special glands. It protects and lubricates delicate surfaces, including the inside of the nose.

Nasal cavity: space in the skull, behind the nose, through which inhaled air passes on its way to the lungs.

Nerve fiber: special cell capable of passing an electrical signal, or nerve impulse, along its thread-like length.

Olfactory organs: the organs of smell, positioned in the top of the nasal cavity.

Papillae: small bumps on the surface of the tongue on which the taste buds are positioned.

Pheromones: chemical messengers which cause a response in the organs of smell. Pheromones are produced in our perspiration, but we are not normally conscious of their presence.

Proprioceptor: microscopic organ which detects the stretching in a muscle or tendon. It allows the brain to be aware of the exact position of our limbs.

Receptor: structure which responds to a stimulus such as touch or smell, and causes a nerve impulse to be generated.

Reflex: automatic response of the body to a stimulus. This allows a rapid response without involving the brain.

Many reflexes serve to protect us from a possibly dangerous stimulus.

Soft palate: soft tissue at the back of the roof of the mouth. The soft palate can divert air to go through the mouth or through the nasal area as required. It also seals off the nasal passages as we swallow.

Spinal cord: thick bundle of nerve fibers running up the spine, and joining on to the brain.

Stimulus: an event which can cause a response in the nervous system, such as pain, touch, heat, etc.

Taste buds: groups of taste receptor cells in the mouth, mostly on the tongue.

Tendon: tough ropy material which connects muscle to bone.

Thalamus: small area in the brain through which most of the information received from the sense organs passes.

Turbinates: Thin shelves of bone in the nasal cavity which guide the air and direct its flow.

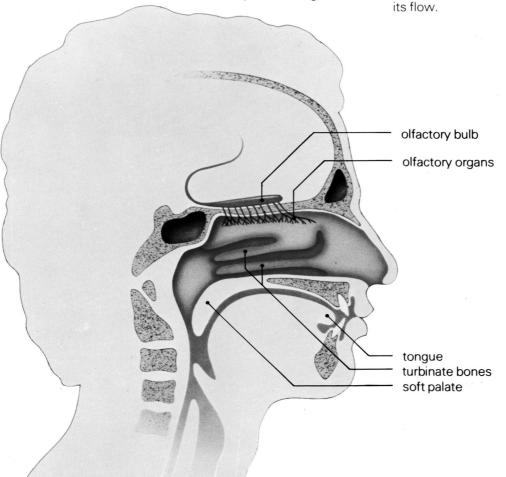

olfactory bulb

olfactory organs

tongue

turbinate bones

soft palate

Index

Braille 12, 38
brain 6, 8, 9, 10, 14, 15, 16, 20, 22, 23, 24, 25, 26, 34, 35, 36

cilia 26, 27, 38
cortex 8, 9, 38

fingertips 9, 12, 16, 17, 18
food 6, 7, 10, 24, 34

ganglia 20, 38

hairs, on skin 12

joint 22

leprosy 14, 38

mercaptan 30, 38
mouth 16, 24, 32, 34, 35
mucus 26, 27, 36, 38
muscles 10, 14, 22, 23

nasal cavity 24, 26, 28, 38
nerve 8, 12, 14, 18, 20, 22, 25, 29, 30, 35
nerve fiber 9, 10, 26, 38

olfactory organs 26, 27, 38

pain 10, 11, 14, 18–19, 20, 21, 34, 35
papillae 32, 33, 38
pheromones 30, 38
pressure 10, 11, 12, 14, 18, 19
proprioceptor 22, 23, 38

receptor 10, 11, 12, 13, 14, 16, 18, 20, 22, 23, 25, 26, 27, 28, 29, 30, 32, 35, 39
reflex 23, 39

saliva 24, 34
skin 10–11, 12, 14, 16, 18, 19
smell 6, 7, 8, 9, 24, 25, 26, 27, 28, 30, 31, 34, 36, 37
soft palate 24, 26, 27, 32, 39
spinal cord 20, 23, 39
stimulus 10, 39

taste 6, 7, 9, 24, 25, 32, 33, 34, 36
taste bud 32, 33, 34, 39
temperature 6, 7, 10, 14, 16–17, 18
tendon 14, 22, 23, 39
thalamus 8, 39
tongue 12, 25, 32, 33, 34
touch 6, 7, 8, 9, 10, 11, 12, 13, 14, 15, 18
turbinates 26, 39